This Land Is Your Land

by **Tamera Bryant**

This Land Is Your Land
   by Tamera Bryant

Illustrations by Burgandy Beam
Photography: p.1 © W. Cody/CORBIS; p.2 © Kevin Fleming/CORBIS; p.3 © Lee Snider; Lee Snider/CORBIS; p.4 © CORBIS; p.5 © Lee Snider; Lee Snider/CORBIS; p.6 © Francis G. Mayer/CORBIS; p.7 © Barry Winiker/Index Stock/Imagery/PictureQuest; p.9 © CORBIS; p.11 top © Photo courtesy of Scott Dean; p.11 bottom © CORBIS; p.13 © Philip Gould/CORBIS; p.14 © David Smart/Stock South/PictureQuest; p.15 © Dave G. Houser/CORBIS; p.17 © CORBIS; p.19 © Richard A. Cooke/CORBIS; p.20 © Photograph courtesy of Dean Robinson; p.22 © Dorothy Molter Museum; p.23 © Dorothy Molter Museum; p.25 © Jeff Vanuga/CORBIS; p.27 top © Bettmann/CORBIS; p.27 bottom © State Historical Society of North Dakota Conserv. 12–10; p.28 © CORBIS; p.29 © Nathan Benn/CORBIS; p.31 top © Bettmann/CORBIS; p.31 bottom © Dave G. Houser/CORBIS; p.33 © Danny Lehman/CORBIS; p.37 top © Academy of Natural Sciences of Philadelphia/CORBIS; p.37 bottom © Liz Hymans/CORBIS; p.38 © Burstein Collection/CORBIS; p.39 © Danny Lehman/CORBIS; p.41 © Macduff Everton/CORBIS; p.42 © Photograph courtesy of Kevin Boos; p.43 © Photograph courtesy of Kevin Boos; p.44 © Buddy Mays/CORBIS; p.45 © David Muench/CORBIS; p.47 © Bill Ross/ CORBIS; p.48 © Pat O'Hara/CORBIS; p.49 © Tom Bean/CORBIS; p.50 © Wolfgang Kaehler/CORBIS; p.51 © David Muench/CORBIS; p.52 © Ray Krantz/CORBIS; p.53 © Joe Williamson Collection, Puget Sound Maritime Historical Society, Seattle, Washington

Nonfiction Reviewer
   John Barell, Ed.D.
   Educational Consultant, The American Museum of Natural History
   New York City

Design, Production, and Art Buying by
   Inkwell Publishing Solutions, Inc., New York City
Cover Design by
   Inkwell Publishing Solutions, Inc., New York City

ISBN: 0-7367-1784-6

Copyright © Zaner-Bloser, Inc.

All rights reserved. No part of this book may be reproduced or transmitted in any form or by any means, electronic or mechanical, including photocopying, recording, or by any information storage and retrieval system, without permission in writing from the Publisher.

Web sites have been carefully researched for accuracy, content, and appropriateness. However, Web sites are subject to change. Internet usage should always be monitored.

Zaner-Bloser, Inc., P.O. Box 16764, Columbus, Ohio 43216-6764, 1-800-421-3018

Printed in China
04 05 06 07 (321) 5 4 3 2

TABLE OF CONTENTS

Introduction:
This Land Is Your Land iv

Chapter 1: The Northeastern States.. 1
The *Kalmar Nyckel*,
  Delaware 2
Harriet Tubman Home,
  New York 4
Hugh Moore Park,
  Pennsylvania 6
For More Information 8

Chapter 2: The Southeastern States.. 9
Florewood River Plantation,
  Mississippi 10
Plaquemine Locks,
  Louisiana 12
W.C. Handy Home,
  Tennessee 14
For More Information 16

Chapter 3: The Great Lakes Region. 17
Cahokia Mounds State
  Historic Site, Illinois 18
Bridgeton Mill, Indiana..... 20
Dorothy Molter Museum,
  Minnesota 22
For More Information 24

Chapter 4: The Northern Plains.... 25
Sakakawea Monument,
  North Dakota 26

Mark Twain Birthplace State
  Historic Site, Missouri ... 28
Willa Cather Pioneer
  Memorial, Nebraska..... 30
For More Information 32

Chapter 5: The Southwest 33
Kartchner Caverns State Park,
  Arizona............... 34
San Jose de los Jemez State
  Monument, New Mexico . 36
Sequoyah's Cabin,
  Oklahoma............. 38
For More Information 40

Chapter 6: The Mountain States ... 41
Rock Creek Station, Idaho... 42
Newspaper Rock State
  Historical Monument,
  Utah 44
For More Information 46

Chapter 7: The Pacific States 47
Totem Bight, Alaska 48
Astoria Column, Oregon.... 50
The *Arthur Foss*, Washington 52
The *Virginia V*, Washington .. 53
For More Information 54

Glossary 55
Index 56

iii

INTRODUCTION
This Land Is Your Land

History is about movement, about how things change.

A river changes its course. A settlement becomes a city. A wagon path becomes a superhighway.

History is also about how things stay the same. Fields of grass still grow in Nebraska, as they have for centuries. Ships still sail the Atlantic, although they look a little different from the way they used to look. People also stay the same. People still make mistakes, although they can learn from them. And people still go out of their way to help one another.

This book is about history. It's about America's ancestors and the land that helped shape this nation. It's about the people and places we choose to remember and treasure. They belong to all of us, including you.

This book offers a quick look at America's heritage. You will visit the Pacific Coast and the Mississippi Delta. You will travel across the vast Great Plains. You will meet cowboys from the Wild West, along with talented writers. As you read, think about where our nation has been, where we are, and where we're going.

Think about where you're going, too. Maybe you'd like to go to one of the places in this book!

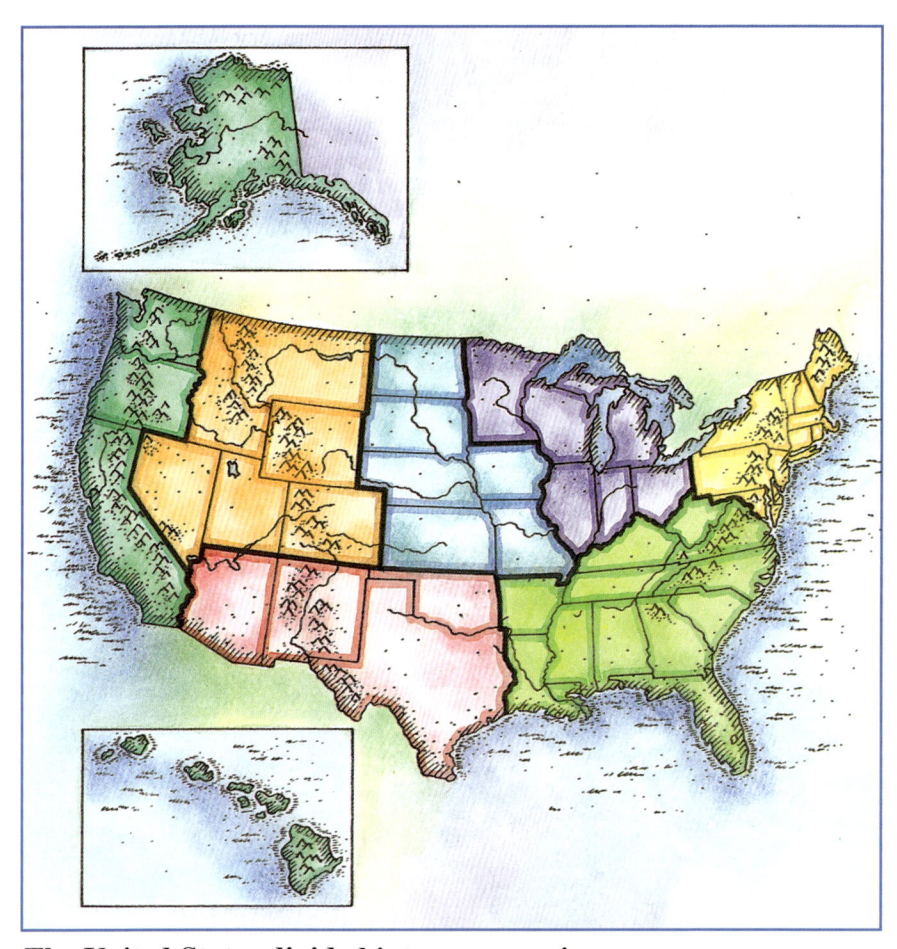

The United States divided into seven regions

Chapter 1
The Northeastern States

I saw a ship a-sailing,
A-sailing on the sea.
And, oh, but it was laden
With pretty things for thee.
There were comfits in the cabin,
And apples in the hold;
The sails were made of silk,
And the masts were all of gold.
—from *The Real Mother Goose,*
  Rand McNally & Company

Kalmar Nyckel
Delaware

Who built the first log cabins in America? It wasn't the Pilgrims. It was the settlers who arrived on the *Kalmar Nyckel*.

The *Kalmar Nyckel* first sailed from Sweden to America in 1637. It carried twenty-five settlers. They were all men. Some came from Sweden and Holland. Some came from Finland and Germany. One came from the Caribbean. They spoke different languages, so they probably had trouble talking with each other. Still, they banded together. After they arrived in America, they built the first log cabins here, in what is now the state of Delaware.

Then the *Kalmar Nyckel* sailed back to Sweden. It returned to America three more times. Each time it brought more

The rebuilt *Kalmar Nyckel*

settlers. They included women and children. This ship made more trips than any other settlers' ship of that time.

The *Kalmar Nyckel* sank in the late 1600s. An exact model of it was built 350 years after it first landed here in 1638. The *Kalmar Nyckel* sailed again in 1997. Thousands of people cheered it.

Today this ship spreads good will for the state of Delaware. It sails from Virginia to New York. If you live in this area, you might have seen it.

The *Kalmar Nyckel* not only delights its visitors. It also reminds us that we can be different and still work together.

Kalmar Nyckel **Monument**

Harriet Tubman Home
Auburn, New York

What kind of conductor does not ride a train? Harriet Tubman could have told you.

Harriet Tubman escaped from slavery in 1849 and made it her life's work to help other slaves escape. She became a conductor on the Underground Railroad. This railroad had no train. It was a group of people who lived in many states. They worked together to help slaves escape from the South to the North, where they could be free.

Over 11 years, Tubman made 19 trips to the South. Each time, she brought people back to the North with her, leading more than 300 slaves to freedom.

Harriet Tubman

During the Civil War, she worked as a nurse, cook, scout, and spy for the Union Army. After the war, she moved to Auburn, New York. William H. Seward, a U.S. senator from New York, sold her a house. At that time, it was illegal to sell a house to a black person, but he did it anyway.

Harriet Tubman died in 1913. Her home stood empty for many years. In 1944, the city wanted to tear it down, but the A.M.E. Zion Church raised enough money to save it.

Today, Harriet Tubman's home is a memorial to her life and work. If you visit there, you can see some of her furniture and other belongings. Imagine what it would be like to walk where she walked. You can stand in a place of history.

Harriet Tubman's Home

Hugh Moore Park
Easton, Pennsylvania

How did people transport goods like coal and lumber in the late eighteenth century? There were no trucks or trains. Wagons couldn't carry much, and they were slow.

Canal boats were the answer. So, with shovels and sweat, people dug thousands of miles of canals. The canals were connected with **locks**.

Pennsylvania had 1,356 miles of canals. That was more than any other state. These water highways connected farms, cities, factories, and mines. The boats that traveled them carried people, animals, and goods.

Illustration of a mule-drawn canal boat

Modern-day mule-drawn canal boat

The Lehigh Canal was part of Pennsylvania's canal system. Boats traveled up and down this system. Many of them carried coal from Pennsylvania mines. They were taking it to Philadelphia and New York City.

A long rope linked each boat to mules on the bank. The mules pulled the boats from place to place. At Hugh Moore Park you can ride one of these mule-drawn boats. The *Josiah White II* is still operating. You can also visit the Locktender's House Museum and the restored locks.

For More Information

Hill, Lee Sullivan. *Canals Are Water Roads.* Carolrhoda, 1997.

Mulligan, Kate. *Canal Parks, Museums and Characters of the Mid-Atlantic.* Wakefield Press, 1999.

Schotter, Roni. *F Is for Freedom.* DK Publishing, 2000.

Spangenburg, Ray, and Diane Moser. *American Historic Places: Political and Social Movements.* Facts on File, 1998.

Sullivan, George. *Harriet Tubman.* Scholastic, 2002.

Wilbur, Keith. *Tall Ships of the World.* Chelsea House, 1997.

Chapter 2
The Southeastern States

I wish I was in the land of cotton

Old times there are not forgotten

Look away! Look away!

Look away, Dixieland.

—traditional, by Daniel Decatur Emmett

Florewood River Plantation
Greenwood, Mississippi

New machines usually make work easier. How could the invention of a new machine increase the need for slave labor?

By the early 1800s, the new cotton gin was quickly removing the seeds from cotton. This meant that cloth could be made faster than ever. Northern cloth makers needed lots of cotton. They wanted to keep the machines busy. Soon Southern planters were growing cotton in all their fields. They used slave labor to work the fields. Then they sold the cotton to Northern cloth makers. The owners of large cotton plantations got rich.

Cotton became the South's biggest business. Mississippi produced more cotton than any other state. The Florewood River Plantation in Greenwood, Mississippi, once grew cotton. Now it is a living history museum. You can see what life was like during this time in our history, for the planter and for the slaves.

The planter's mansion is the largest building here. The kitchen is a separate building. This kept the main house from getting too hot and helped to prevent fires.

You can also see the small houses where the slaves lived. One building served as both a church and a schoolhouse. There is also a tool shed and a blacksmith's shop, along with barns and a mill to grind grain. Tour guides can tell you many details about life on a cotton plantation.

Florewood River Plantation

The Cotton Gin

Plaquemine Locks
Plaquemine, Louisiana

Let's say you want to connect two rivers to make it easier for ships to travel from one place to another. However, one river is higher than the other river. How can you connect them? By building a canal lock.

Canal locks are large water chambers. They move ships from high water to low water and from low water to high water. To picture how this works, imagine that a ship is moving from a high river to a lower one.

First, the ship moves into the lock. Gates close on both ends of the chamber. Water pours out of the chamber. As the water level lowers, the ship lowers with it. After a while, the water in the chamber reaches the same level as the water in the lower river. Then the front gate opens, and the ship moves into the lower river.

Illustration of a ship moving through a canal lock

The Plaquemine Lockhouse

Water has always been important in Louisiana. Bayous, lakes, and rivers run throughout the state. However, they are not all connected. The Plaquemine Canal Lock connected a large **bayou** to the Mississippi River. The lock made travel easier and faster.

Plaquemine opened in 1909 and operated for 52 years. The opening of the locks meant increased trade and commerce. A more modern set of locks was built at Port Allen in 1961. Then the old lock was shut down. Today you can visit the site. Inside the lockhouse is a museum. While you're there, climb the 40-foot tower. You will have a great view of the mighty Mississippi River.

W.C. Handy Home
Memphis, Tennessee

How could the blues make someone happy? Blues music certainly helped raise the spirits of African Americans working in the cotton fields. Blues music tells of the hardships of the day and the hope of better days to come. It is heartfelt, soulful, and inspirational. As African Americans moved to Memphis in the early 1900s, they brought the blues with them.

Clubs and theaters sprang up along Beale Street in Memphis. Blues musicians, including W.C. Handy, played in these clubs. His 1912 song "Memphis Blues" was his first song to be recorded. Today, Handy is known as "Father of the Blues." Beale Street is called the "Home of the Blues."

W.C. Handy Park is on Beale Street. A statue of Handy watches over the blues musicians who still play in the park. Listeners leave tips to show their appreciation to the musicians.

Statue of W.C. Handy

The W.C. Handy home

This tiny two-room house was W.C. Handy's home. He lived here with his wife and six children. In this house, he wrote "Memphis Blues," "Yellow Dog Blues," and "Beale Street Blues." Several of Handy's personal belongings are on display. The house also serves as headquarters of The Blues Foundation.

Try listening to a recording of W.C. Handy's blues. How does it make you feel?

For More Information

Elmer, Howard. *Blues: Its Birth and Growth*. Rosen, 1999.

Hill, Lee Sullivan. *Canals Are Water Roads*. Carolrhoda, 1997.

Kalman, Bobbie. *Life on a Plantation*. Crabtree, 1997.

Spangenburg, Ray, and Diane Moser. *American Historic Places: Literature and the Arts*. Facts on File, 1997.

Summer, L.S. *W.C. Handy: Father of the Blues*. Child's World, 2001.

Check your local library for blues recordings. Try other blues artists, too, such as B.B. King, T-Bone Walker, Ma Rainey, Stevie Ray Vaughan, and Bonnie Raitt.

CHAPTER 3
The Great Lakes Region

Come all you bold sailors that follow the Lakes,
On an iron ore vessel your living to make;
I shipped in Chicago, bid adieu to the shore,
Bound away to Escanaba for red iron ore.
Derry down down, derry down.
Derry down down, derry down.

—a traditional Great Lakes shanty

Cahokia Mounds State Historic Site
Collinsville, Illinois

When you think of Illinois, do you think of very old, or even lost, civilizations? Probably not, but you should!

The old city of Cahokia thrived from about A.D. 700 to 1400. It covered nearly six square miles just west of what is now Collinsville, Illinois. Cahokia was the most advanced society north of Mexico.

In this city, the houses were built in rows and around open plazas. Dirt mounds served as burial places. Some mounds were shaped like cones, while others had flat tops. At one time, there were more than 120 mounds here. The king and his servants lived on top of the largest mound. Grain fields stretched outside the city.

No one is certain what happened to the Cahokia people. However, by A.D. 1400, they were gone.

Illustration of old city of Cahokia

18

Stairway leading to Monks Mound

Monks Mound (Mound 38) is the largest one at Cahokia. It covers 16 acres and is 100 feet tall. To create the mounds, workers used stone tools, digging sticks, and their hands. They carried dirt to the mounds in woven baskets. Scientists estimate that it took 15,000,000 baskets of dirt to build Monks Mound. Can you imagine helping to carry that much dirt?

If you visit, you can climb the steps to the top of the mound. From there, you can see all the other mounds. Maybe you will figure out what happened to the Cahokia people!

Bridgeton Mill
Parke County, Indiana

How many different things can you grind in a mill? The people at Bridgeton Mill in Parke County, Indiana, know.

The Bridgeton Mill started out as a sawmill in a log cabin. It ran on waterpower from a nearby river. As more people moved into the area, they needed flour and cornmeal. The mill was rerigged so it could become a **gristmill** and grind grains. In the 1890s, a new roller milling process was installed so the mill could make flour.

Then in 1951, a dust explosion nearly destroyed the mill. It was repaired and reopened as a feed mill. This time, the mill was powered by electricity. In 1969, the feed mill was closed. French Burr stones, stones from Paris which were thought to

Bridgeton Mill

be the best for milling flour, were installed. Those stones are still used today to grind flour. Bridgeton is a gristmill again! Visitors can watch the French Burr stones at work. Each stone is 48 inches around. These powerful stones grind wheat into flour and corn into meal. You can feel the floor vibrate when the stones are grinding.

Today the Bridgeton Mill is a beautiful site. If you stop there, you can buy six kinds of cornmeal: black, white, red, blue, yellow, and roasted. You can also buy six kinds of flour. Just don't ask for pine boards or feed for your cattle because this mill doesn't make those things—right now!

On your way to the mill, be sure to drive through some of the 32 covered bridges in Parke County. If you visit in October, you can enjoy the Parke County Covered Bridge Festival, too.

Dorothy Molter Museum
Ely, Minnesota

Why would anyone make a fence out of broken canoe paddles? Dorothy Molter must have had a very good reason.

She lived on Knife Lake near the border of Minnesota and Canada. Canoe paddlers on the lake had a special name for Dorothy: the "Root Beer Lady." It's no wonder. She made more than 11,000 bottles of root beer each year. She shared them with visitors who stopped by. Dorothy was also a nurse. She provided first aid for campers and hikers.

Dorothy died in 1986, but many people remember her flower gardens. The bright fences around them were made from broken canoe paddles. Folks gladly gave her their paddles. It was an honor to have a paddle in Dorothy's fence. She is remembered as an independent, **hospitable,** and inspirational woman.

Dorothy Molter

Paddle fence at Dorothy's home

    Winters on the lake were cold. Dorothy spent those months in her winter cabin. In spring, she moved to a different cabin. This summer cabin was more like a tent.
    After Dorothy's death, her cabins were torn down. Pieces were loaded onto dogsleds and snowmobiles. They were moved to Moose Lake and then to downtown Ely, Minnesota. Volunteers rebuilt both cabins. They are now open for visitors again. Dorothy would want it that way, don't you think?

For More Information

Bruun, Erik. *Minnesota*. Black Dog and Leventhal, 2002.

Chappell, Sally Anderson. *Cahokia: Mirror of the Cosmos*. University of Chicago Press, 2002.

Donohoe, Kitty. *Bunyan and Banjoes: Michigan Songs and Stories*. Thunder Bay, 1997.

Searcy, Margaret Zehmer. *Ikwa of the Mound-Builder Indians*. Firebird Press, 1989.

Soetebier, Virginia. *Woman of the Green Glade: The Story of an Ojibway Woman on the Great Lakes Frontier*. McDonald and Woodward, 2000.

Spangenburg, Ray, and Diane Moser. *American Historic Places: Science and Invention*. Facts on File, 1997.

CHAPTER 4
The Northern Plains

Oh, give me a home

Where the buffalo roam,

Where the deer and the antelope play.

Where seldom is heard a discouraging word

And the skies are not cloudy all day.

—*Home on the Range,* traditional cowboy song

Sakakawea Monument
Bismarck, North Dakota

Have you heard about the Lewis and Clark expedition? They were explorers sent by President Thomas Jefferson to search out a land route to the Pacific Ocean and to gather information about the West. However, Lewis and Clark needed a guide in this new territory. Who did they turn to?

Sakakawea (also spelled Sacajawea) was a Native American from the Shoshone tribe. In 1804, she and her husband joined Lewis and Clark on their famous expedition. Her husband was the team's **interpreter**. He helped Lewis and Clark understand the Native American languages they encountered. Soon, Sakakawea became an important member of the team.

Sakakawea knew the land. This made her a valuable guide. She also knew which plants were safe to eat. She knew which plants could be used as medicines. She spoke English and could also help translate the Shoshone language.

In 1905, the Women's Clubs of North Dakota wanted to honor Sakakawea. They decided to build a statue. The clubs raised more than $3,500. School children also saved pennies. They gave $555.78. The statue they built is 12 feet high and stands on the capitol grounds in Bismarck.

Sakakawea and her husband had a son who was born during the trip. The statue shows Sakakawea with her baby strapped to her back. She is looking westward toward the land she helped explore.

Painting of Sakakawea leading Lewis and Clark

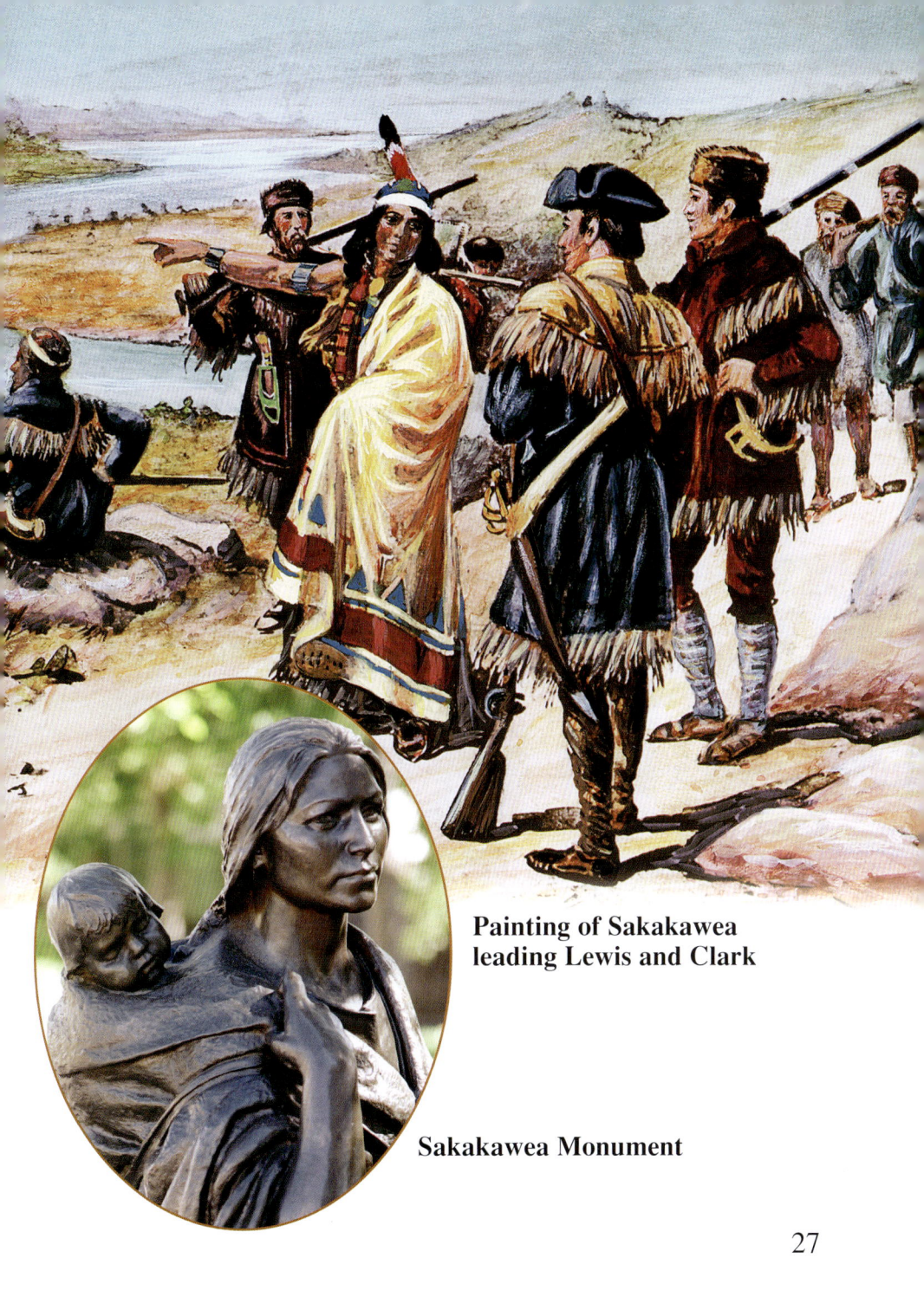

Sakakawea Monument

27

Mark Twain Birthplace State Historic Site
Florida, Missouri

Have you read *The Adventures of Tom Sawyer* or *Huckleberry Finn*? They are the two most famous books by Samuel Clemens. Who is that, you ask?

Samuel Clemens is the birth name of Mark Twain. Clemens first called himself Mark Twain when he was a newspaper reporter. He also spent time as a printer and an editor. In addition, he received his license to become a Mississippi River boat pilot when he was 23. Some say he was the greatest American writer ever.

Mark Twain was born in 1835 in Missouri. He loved to spend time on his uncle's farm there. He listened to one of the farm workers tell stories. That man, Uncle Dan'l, became a character in *Huckleberry Finn*.

Portrait of Samuel Clemens (Mark Twain)

Mark Twain's life started in a tiny two-room cabin. At that time, the cabin was home to the family of eight. It is now part of a museum. Twain's furniture decorates the cabin, which was moved from its original spot. A red granite monument marks its first location in the town of Florida, Missouri.

If you go to the museum, you can visit a library that holds first editions of Twain's books. You can see a copy of *The Adventures of Tom Sawyer* that he wrote by hand. Can you imagine how long that took?

Some copies of Twain's first editions

Willa Cather Pioneer Memorial Red Cloud, Nebraska

A marker in Webster County, Nebraska, says:

"The history of every country begins in the heart of a man or a woman. The history of this land began in the heart of Willa Cather."

Willa Cather lived from 1873 until 1947. Can you guess what kind of work she did? She was an author. She wrote about the history of this land in a way that touched many people.

At the age of nine, Cather moved to Nebraska from Virginia. The vast prairie was nothing like her home, but she soon grew to love it. She admired the hard-working people she met. These are the people she wrote about later.

Willa Cather wrote twelve novels. Her book titled *One of Ours* won the Pulitzer Prize. It was about a Nebraska farm boy who served in World War I.

Six of her books are set in Webster County. That is the place that Cather knew and loved. The western half of that county is now known as Catherland.

Many of the sites that appear in Cather's novels and stories are still there. Banks, homes, stores, and churches are part of this huge memorial. Many have been restored. The house on page 31 is the one where Cather grew up. Can you imagine life on the prairie? How do you think it would have been different from the way people live today?

Portrait of Willa Cather and the house where she grew up

31

For More Information

Bannan, Jan. *The West Less Traveled*. Fulcrum, 1996.

Bedard, Michael. *The Divide*. Bantam, 1997.

Collins, David. *Mark T-W-A-I-N!: A Story About Samuel Clemens*. Carolrhoda, 1993.

Kalman, Bobbie. *Nations of the Plains*. Crabtree, 2001.

MacLachlan, Patricia. *Sarah, Plain and Tall*. HarperCollins, 1985.

Spangenburg, Ray, and Diane Moser. *American Historic Places: Literature and the Arts*. Facts on File, 1997.

Wooten, Sara McIntosh. *Willa Cather: Writer of the Prairie*. Enslow, 1998.

Chapter 5
The Southwest

Through rocky arroyos so dark and so deep
Down the sides of the mountains so slippery and steep
You've good judgment, sure-footed, wherever you go
You're a safety conveyance, my little Chopo.

Chopo my pony, Chopo my pride
Chopo my amigo, Chopo I'll ride.
From Mexico's borders 'cross Texas Llanos
To the salt Peco River I ride you Chopo.

— traditional

Kartchner Caverns State Park
Benson, Arizona

Have you ever heard of a "living cave"? What do you think it means?

Kartchner Caverns were formed by water. For thousands of years, rainwater has trickled through the soil above the caverns. It is dissolving some of the rock underground. Slowly, small passages and large chambers have formed in the rock.

This huge limestone cave already has 13,000 feet of passages. Two of the rooms are as long as football fields. Their walls glisten with crystals. **Stalactites** hang down from the ceiling like icicles. They are made of the mineral deposits in the dripping water. **Stalagmites** form under the dripping stalactites. They grow up from the floor. Some stalactites and stalagmites have joined in the middle. They form columns up to 100 feet high.

Kartchner Caverns is a "living" cave. That means that it is still growing. Water is still trickling, and mineral deposits are still forming on the ceilings and floors. The temperature inside stays around 68°F most of the time. The humidity stays near 99 percent.

If you visit this cave, you can see one of the longest "soda straw" stalactites in the world. It is more than 21 feet long. A soda straw stalactite is hollow. This one is still dripping water and growing longer.

Kartchner Caverns

San Jose de los Jemez State Monument
Jemez, New Mexico

When is a ruin a good thing? The answer: when it means the end of slavery.

In 1598, Spaniards came north from Mexico and moved into what is now New Mexico. Their plan was to start a new colony for Spain. The Spaniards quickly conquered the Pueblo people, who had lived in the area for over 200 years. The Pueblos were Native Americans.

The Pueblo people were forced to work as slaves. They lost their farms. They were not allowed to practice their own religion. The Spaniards built **missions** throughout the area. They used the missions to teach their religion to the Pueblo people.

The Spanish built the mission at Jemez. For 80 years, it was home to privileged Spaniards. It was jail to the Pueblo people. However, by 1680, the Pueblo people had had enough. They rose up and drove the Spaniards out of their lands. They took back what was theirs.

The ruins of the Mission at Jemez

Ruins of other Spanish missions are scattered across New Mexico. The ruins at Jemez, however, are among the most impressive in the Southwest. If you go there, be sure to visit the library. There you can learn more about the Pueblos' struggle to regain their land. Can you imagine how much courage they had, and what they had to do to succeed?

Jemez Governor in native dress

Sequoyah's Cabin
Sallisaw, Oklahoma

What would our lives be like without an alphabet? How would we record our thoughts and ideas? What would we know about our history?

Sequoyah faced this problem in the early 1800s. He was a Native American of the Cherokee tribe. He had often watched white people read and write. He wanted his people to read and write, too. Yet, the Cherokee had no alphabet. Sequoyah decided to make one. By 1812, he had succeeded.

Sequoyah's alphabet had 85 characters. Each one stood for a sound in the Cherokee language. The alphabet caught on quickly. Within a few months, many Cherokee were reading and writing. In 1828, the Cherokee published a newspaper. It was the first Native American newspaper in the United States.

Artist's rendering of Sequoyah

The cabin where Sequoyah worked and lived is now inside a stone building. It is part of a museum. If you go inside, you will find a typewriter. The keys do not have letters on them. They have Sequoyah's characters.

Thousands of people learned to read and write because of Sequoyah. He helped to preserve the Cherokee culture. The giant sequoia trees were named to honor him. Sequoia National Park in California was also named for him.

Building at Sequoyah's homesite

For More Information

Bannan, Jan. *The West Less Traveled.* Fulcrum, 1996.

Delafosse, Claude. *Caves: Hidden World.* Cartwheel, 2000.

Flanagan, Alice. *The Pueblos: A True Book.* Children's Press, 1998.

Freedman, Russell. *In the Days of the Vaqueros: America's First True Cowboys.* Clarion, 2001.

Jones, Oscar, and Joy Jones. *Historic Hispanic America.* Hippocrene, 1993.

Klausner, Janet. *Sequoyah's Gift: A Portrait of the Cherokee Leader.* HarperCollins, 1993.

Oppenheim, Joanne. *Sequoyah: Cherokee Hero.* Troll, 1979.

Chapter 6:
The Mountain States

As I walked out one morning for pleasure,
I met a cowpuncher a jogging along;
His hat was throwed back and his spurs was a jingling,
And as he advanced he was singing this song.
Yippee Ti Yi Yo, get along little dogies
It's your misfortune and none of my own
Yippee Ti Yi Yo, get along little dogies
For you know that Wyoming will soon be your home.

—*Git Along, Little Dogies*, traditional cowboy song

Rock Creek Station
near Kimberley, Idaho

Can you imagine crossing the desert long ago? There were no fast-food restaurants or other places to get a snack. There was no water, anywhere.

For centuries, Rock Creek was a welcome stop for travelers. In the middle of the desert, this creek was one of the few places where people could find water. In the 1840s, pioneers on the Oregon Trail camped here. It also served as a station for drivers on the Overland Stage Line. In 1865, the Rock Creek Store was built. A post office was added in 1871.

Rock Creek Station

The Stricker House cellar at Rock Creek

   The Rock Creek Store is still standing. North of the store are two cellars. They were both used for storage, and sometimes one served as a jail.
   The Herman Stricker House also stands here. Herman and his wife Lucy moved to Rock Creek in 1876 and built this house in 1900. The upper floor was a hotel for cowboys, travelers, and engineers. What do you think it was like to spend the night there?

Newspaper Rock State Historical Monument near Monticello, Utah

How can you tell a story with a rock? Ancient Native Americans may have found a way.

The Navajo call Newspaper Rock "Tse 'Hane'." That means "rock that tells a story." The rock, found near Monticello, Utah, is covered with Native American drawings called **petroglyphs**. They were scratched, rubbed, or etched into the rock. Whoever made the drawings used stone hammers and chisels. Perhaps pieces of flint made some of the marks. In all, the drawings cover 200 square feet of the rock.

Many of the drawings on Newspaper Rock are more than 1500 years old. Do they tell a story? If so, whose story is it? Are they messages—or even warnings—to readers? No one knows for sure.

Many of the etchings are of animals and humans. There are also graphic symbols and designs, but their meanings, too, are unclear.

Look at the petroglyphs from Newspaper Rock. What stories could you tell from them?

Petroglyphs at Newspaper Rock

For More Information

Bannan, Jan. *The West Less Traveled.* Fulcrum, 1996.

Freedman, Russell. *Children of the Wild West.* Clarion, 1990.

Freedman, Russell. *Cowboys of the Wild West.* Clarion, 1990.

Hermes, Patricia. *Westward to Home: Joshua's Diary, The Oregon Trail, 1848.* Scholastic, 2001.

Pelz, Ruth. *Black Heroes of the Wild West.* Open Hand, 1990.

Pelz, Ruth. *Women of the Wild West: Biographies from Many Cultures.* Open Hand, 1994.

Chapter 7
The Pacific States

Will you come with me, my Phyllis dear,

To yon blue mountain free?

Where the blossoms smell the sweetest,

Come rove along with me.

It's every Sunday morning

When I am by your side

We'll jump into the wagon

And we'll take a ride.

—*Wait for the Wagon*, traditional, by R. Bishop Buckley

Totem Bight
Ketchikan, Alaska

Have you ever seen a totem pole? Before there were written languages, the carvings on totem poles told stories. They helped to preserve traditions.

In the early 1900s, many native Alaskans moved to the cities. They left behind their villages and totem poles. In time, forests grew over them. Weather wore them down. Would this part of our history be lost? In 1938, the U.S. Forest Service came to the rescue.

The Forest Service had native artists copy the carvings from the old poles onto new cedar logs. The new poles were painted in the original colors. Native workers also built homes like those of long ago. As they worked, they taught ancient skills to younger Native Americans.

Kodjuk Bird Totem Pole

Totem Bight was once a fishing camp. Today it looks like a Native American village of the past. It includes a clan house and 15 totem poles. (A clan is a group of people descending from a common ancestor.)

A clan house of this size could house 30 to 50 people. Its one large room has a fireplace in the center. Like long ago, housewares and other items are stored under the removable floorboards. Food items hang from wooden beams overhead.

If you visit this village, you can imagine what it was like to live here long ago. Guides will tell you the stories on the totem poles. You might be inspired to make a paper or wooden totem pole of your own!

Part of the clan house at Totem Bight

Astoria Column
Astoria, Oregon

Can a concrete column tell a story? This one does. You start at the bottom of the Astoria Column. Then you keep walking around it, looking at each picture. The pictures tell the story of Astoria. It was the first permanent American settlement west of the Rockies.

The Astoria Column is the only memorial of its kind. It has fourteen pictures in all. They are etched in the concrete. The first shows the wilderness. The next shows the discovery of the Columbia River. A Native American village is in one scene. Four scenes are of Lewis and Clark. Others show Fort Astoria. The last picture shows the Great Northern Railway.

Closeup of Astoria Column

Astoria Column was built in 1926. It is 125 feet high and stands on top of Astoria's highest hill. There are 164 steps inside the column. They wind around it, taking you up to the top. From the top of the column, you can see the Columbia River, Youngs Bay, thick forests, and the Pacific Ocean. You can glimpse Mount St. Helens in the state of Washington, as well as other mountains. You can also see the city of Astoria.

Can you imagine etching these pictures in concrete? What would you have chosen to depict? What story would you tell?

Full photo of Astoria Column

The *Arthur Foss*
Seattle, Washington

In 1933, *Arthur Foss* became a movie star. During World War II, *Arthur Foss* served in the Navy. That sounds like an exciting life, doesn't it? Well, here is a surprise: *Arthur Foss* is a **tugboat**! It starred in the movie *Tugboat Annie*.

This tugboat was built in 1888. First named *Wallowa*, it started out towing ships across the Columbia River. Most of these carried lumber. Later it towed log rafts. This tugboat worked around Puget Sound and the Washington coast. In 1929, it was sold to the Foss Company. That's when it was renamed. Tugboats are an important part of the shipping industry because they are used to move large ships. They are powerful due to their steam or diesel engines. They are very important to **commerce** along the waterways.

The *Arthur Foss* is still running today. It is the only wood-hulled tugboat still operating in the United States that was built in the nineteenth century. If you visit Seattle, stop by and take a tour.

The *Arthur Foss*

A photo of the *Virginia V*

The *Virginia V*
Seattle, Washington

At the turn of the century, many small boats sailed around Puget Sound. Some people called them "pointy-enders." Most people called them "mosquito boats." The "Mosquito Fleet" swarmed around the Sound. (A sound is a channel of water that separates an island from the mainland.)

The *Virginia V* was one of these boats. Built in 1921, it carried people and freight between Seattle and Tacoma. It is the only steam-powered mosquito boat left. The *Virginia V* is still running and happy to have visitors.

53

For More Information

Behrens, June. *Missions of the Central Coast.* Lerner, 1997.

Hoyt-Goldsmith, Diane. *Totem Pole.* Holiday House, 1990.

Jones, Veda Boyd. *Native Americans of the Northwest Coast.* Lucent, 2000.

Perham, Molly. *North American Totem Poles: Secrets and Symbols of North America.* Firefly, 1999.

GLOSSARY

bayou (**by**•oo) a marshy inlet or outlet of a river, lake, or gulf; bayous are most common in the southern United States.

commerce (**kom**•uhrs) the buying and selling of goods; trade

gristmill (**grist**•mil) a mill that grinds grains

hospitable (hos•**pi**•tuh•buhl) being generous and kind to one's guests

interpreter (in•**tur**•pri•tuhr) someone who translates languages

locks (**loks**) a system of gates for raising or lowering boats as they pass from one water level to a higher or lower one

missions (**mish**•uhns) churches or other buildings used by missionaries in their work

petroglyphs (**pet**•ruh•glifs) drawings or symbols carved or etched into rock by ancient people

stalactites (stuh•**lak**•tyts) formations that hang from the ceiling of a cave, like an icicle; they are formed by dripping water and mineral deposits.

stalagmites (stuh•**lag**•myts) formations that build up on the ground of a cave and are shaped like a cone; they are formed by dripping water and mineral deposits.

tugboat (**tug**•boht) a small but powerful boat that pushes and pulls ships and barges

INDEX

Listings in **bold** type also appear in the Glossary.

Arthur Foss 52
Astoria Column 50–51
Beale Street 14–15
blues 14–15
Bridgeton Mill 20–21
Cahokia Mounds 18–19
canal 6–7
canal locks 6, 12–13
Cather, Willa 30–31
Catherland 30
Cherokee people 38–39
Civil War 5
Clemens, Samuel 28
cotton 10–11
Father of the Blues 14
Florewood River Plantation 10–11
gristmill 20–21
Handy, W.C. 14–15
Hugh Moore Park 6–7
Kalmar Nyckel 2–3
Kartchner Caverns 34–35
Lewis and Clark 26–27, 50
mission 36–37

56

Molter, Dorothy 22–23
mosquito boat 53
Navajo people 44
Newspaper Rock 44–45
Oregon Trail 42
Overland Stage Line 42
petroglyphs 44–45
Plaquemine Locks 12–13
Pueblo people 36
Rock Creek Station 42–43
Root Beer Lady 22
Sakakawea 26–27
San Jose de los Jemez 36–37
Sequoyah 38–39
Shoshone people 26
stalactite 34
stalagmite 34
Stricker, Herman and Lucy 43
Totem Bight 48–49
totem pole 48–49
Tubman, Harriet 4–5
tugboat 52
Twain, Mark 28–29
Underground Railroad 4
Virginia V 53